Tl
Ch

Mary and Joseph travelled for many, many miles to get from their home in Nazareth to Bethlehem. Mary was tired because she was expecting a baby.

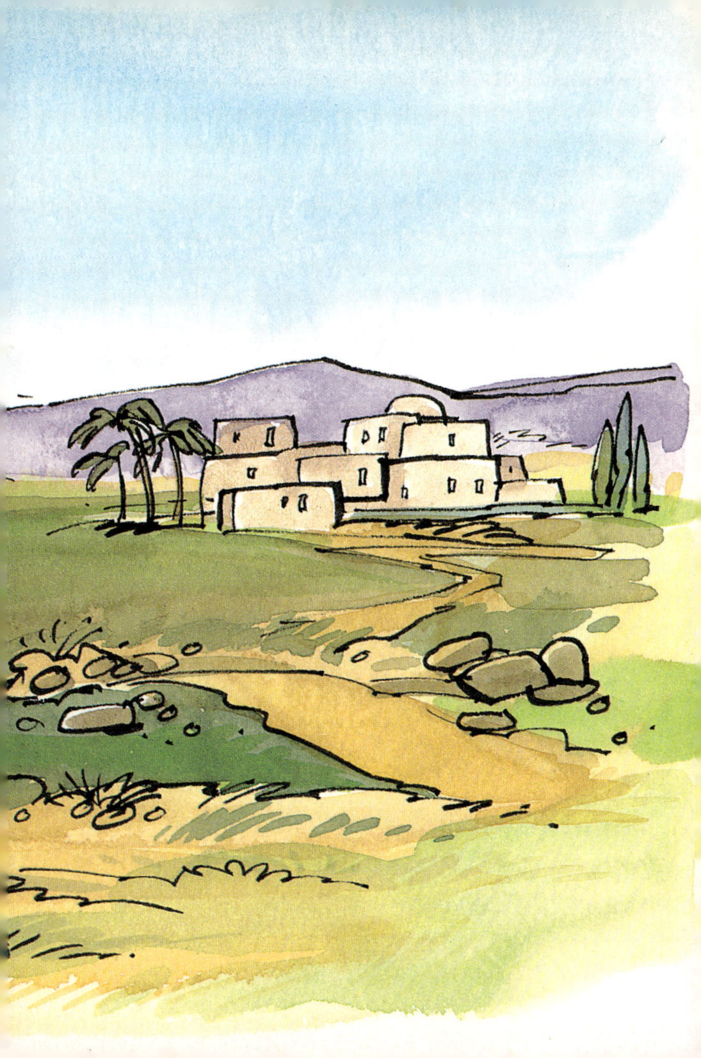

When they reached the town it was full of visitors and there was nowhere for them to stay.

At last they found a kindly innkeeper who agreed to let Mary and Joseph sleep in the stable beside his inn. "It's the best I can do for you," he said. "It's a bit draughty, but at least it's dry."

"Thank you, thank you," sighed Mary.

That night Mary gave birth to a baby boy. She carefully wrapped him in strips of cloth and made a bed for him in the straw-filled manger.

Mary and Joseph looked at the new baby. They knew he was very special. God had sent his angel to tell them both that the baby would be called Jesus – which means Saviour.

High above the stable a very bright star twinkled in the cold night sky.

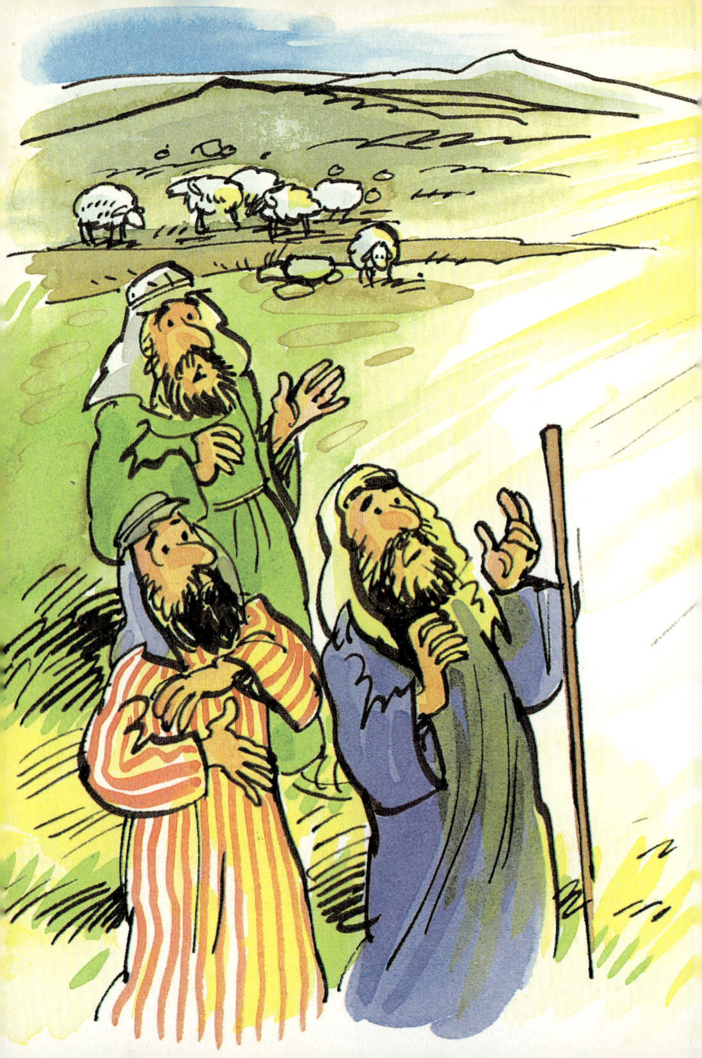

On a nearby hillside there were some shepherds looking after their sheep. Suddenly the sky was filled with a mysterious bright light.

"Don't be afraid!" said an angel above them. "I have some wonderful news for you and for all the world. Tonight a baby has been born in Bethlehem. He is God's own Son, and he will bring peace and joy to all people!"

Suddenly there were millions of angels in the sky, singing praises to God. The shepherds could hardly believe their ears and eyes.

The First Christmas

Open up this re-usable picture.
Decorate it with the stickers in this book!

Now use your stickers!

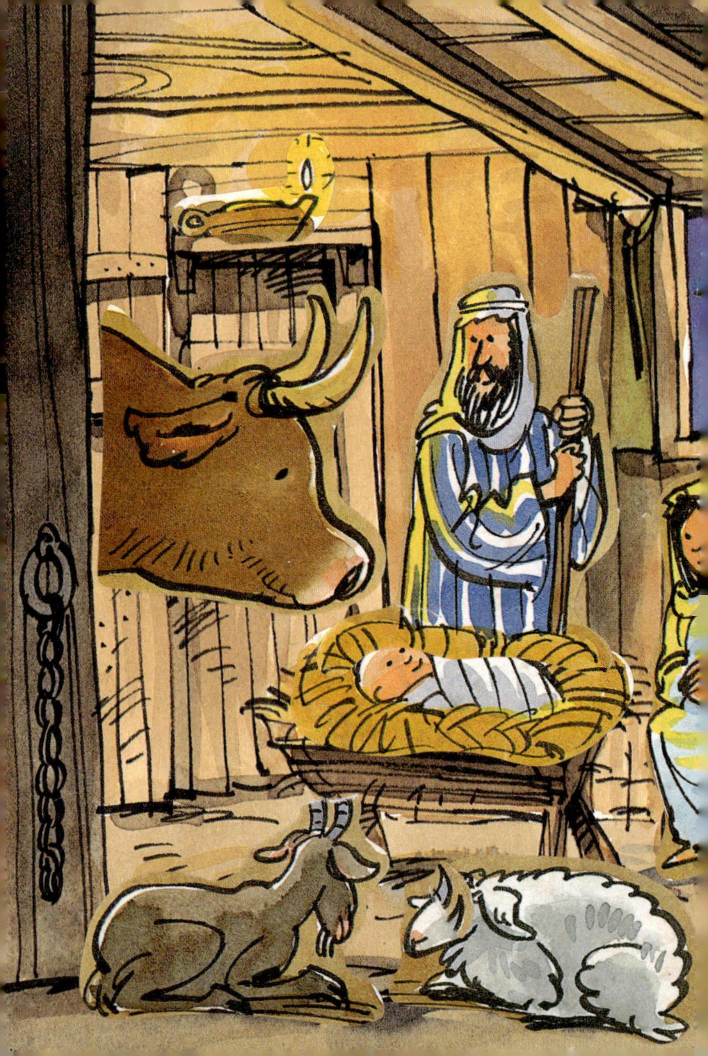

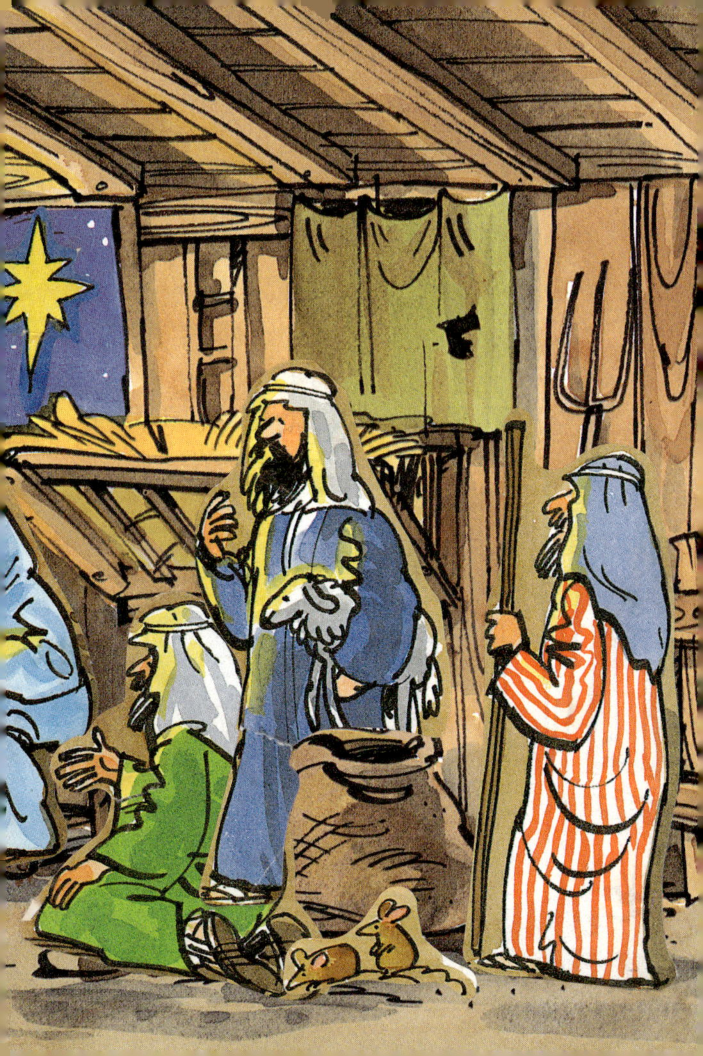

Have fun with your Collect-a-Bible-Story!

1. **Read the whole story.**
2. **Carefully remove the re-usable stickers.**
3. **Complete the picture. Display it in your room!**

Collect the whole series!
Every Collect-a-Bible-Story comes with re-usable stickers and a picture for you to decorate. Make sure you get each one!

When the angels had gone the shepherds leapt to their feet and ran down the hillside. They clattered into the stable where they found the baby Jesus with Mary and Joseph. It was just as the angel had said. The shepherds knelt down in front of the special baby.

Far away, some wise men saw the bright star. They knew it was a special sign that a king had been born. So they travelled to Jerusalem and went to the palace.

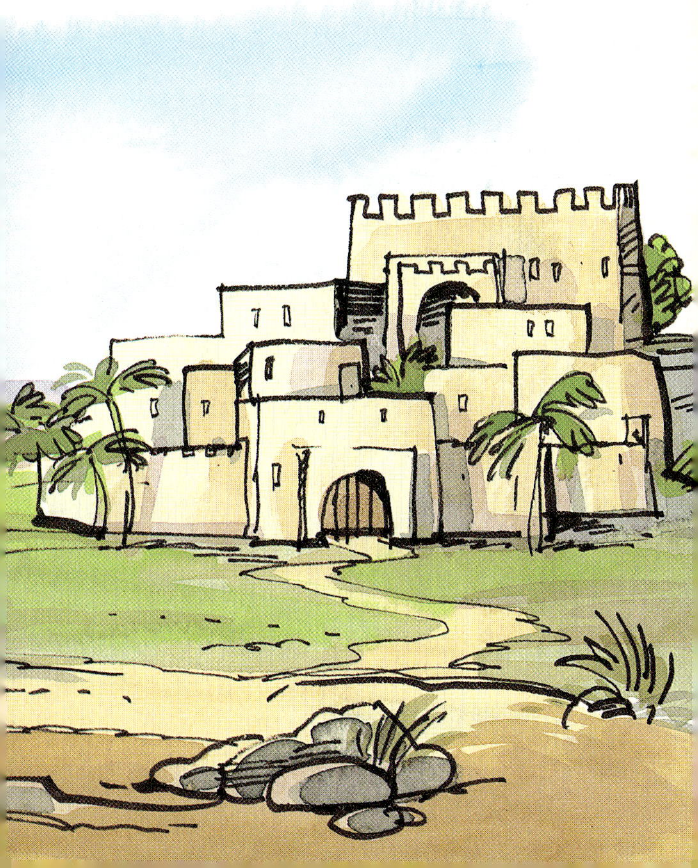

"Where is the new king?" they asked King Herod. "We have come to see him."

Herod was annoyed. He was also worried by this news. Another king? A rival! "You had better keep searching," he said. "When you have found him, let me know. I would like to meet this new king, too." But secretly, Herod planned to find and destroy the baby king.

The wise men continued with their search until, eventually, they reached Mary and Joseph and the child Jesus. They brought some special gifts. Carefully they gave Mary and Joseph their presents of gold, frankincense and myrrh.

"You have a very wonderful child," they whispered. "He will be the most important person the world has ever known!"

Mary held her son tightly as she thought about the things the wise men said.

"Don't tell Herod you have found the new king," an angel warned the wise men as they left Mary and Joseph. So they left the country secretly.

King Herod was furious when he heard about this and everyone was terrified of what he would do next. Mary and Joseph packed up their things and went into Egypt where they would be safe. It was some time before they could return to their own country.